When Adults Hurt Children

Helping Children Heal from Abuse

Written by Marge Eaton Heegaard

To be illustrated by children

Fairview Press, Minneapolis

Published by Fairview Press, 2450 Riverside Avenue, Minneapolis, Minnesota 55454.
Fairview Press is a division of Fairview Health Services, a community-focused health system affiliated with the University of Minnesota, providing a complete range of services, from the prevention of illness and injury to care for the most complex medical conditions.

For a free current catalog of Fairview Press titles, please call toll-free 1-800-544-8207.
Or visit our Web site at www.fairviewpress.org.

ISBN-10: 1-57749-152-1
ISBN-13: 978-1-57749-152-1

First Printing: March 2005
Printed in the United States of America

Cover by Laurie Ingram Design (www.laurieingramdesign.com)
Interior by Dorie McClelland, Spring Book Design (www.springbookdesign.com)

We gratefully acknowledge the following experts for their assistance: Caroline Brennan, Director, Shelter for Abused Women and Children, Naples, Florida; Erin Chadek, CSW, Safe Harbor of Dane County, Wisconsin, and Oasis Counseling Center for Victims of Sexual Abuse; Linda Goldman, LCPC, MS, NBCC, CT in Thanatology, Grief Therapist and Educator, Johns Hopkins University; Donna R. Henne, PhD, Clinical Psychologist; Toni Cavanaugh Johnson, PhD, LCP; JoAnne Kessler, CSW, Family Advocate, Safe Harbor of Dane County, Wisconsin; Janet R. Weisberg, BS, LMT, Certified Traumatologist, Arts in Healing Facilitator.

About this book

This is a book for children ages six through twelve who have been abused. It should be facilitated by an adult trained to work with abused children. The adult will need to be familiar with the pages and skip any page that does not apply to a particular child's situation.

Allow children to illustrate their book with pictures they choose to draw. Children often find it easier to share difficult concerns with pictures than words.

While some children may need help understanding some of the words and concepts in this book, adults can encourage them to make their own decisions about what to draw or write. This will provide children with a sense of empowerment.

Some children may prefer to use markers, but crayons can be more expressive. Older children may use use colored pencils and may add more words. Help children to focus on the expression of their thoughts and feelings rather than their drawing ability.

The art process allows children to express personal feelings symbolically. They may choose to skip a page that is still too painful to deal with. A trained adult should be available to invite a child to talk about his or her drawings. The adult must be able to listen carefully, with empathy.

As children learn to understand and communicate their feelings, they will develop important coping skills and life lessons for healing and survival.

Adults must help children who have been abused.

Children who have been abused need to understand what has happened to them. Abuse must be explained in an age-appropriate way. Children need to know that abuse is never their fault and that they have permission to talk about it.

They need to know that many other children have suffered abuse and neglect. Abuse can happen anywhere. It doesn't matter how much money people have or where they live.

Children need help understanding and expressing the difficult feelings that overwhelm them. They need to grieve their many losses—trust, confidence, self-esteem, hopefulness, even their own home.

Children can learn how to face difficult feelings and cope in healthy ways. A variety of art materials can be provided to help children express their feelings. Clay is excellent for releasing anger. Watercolors are especially good for expressing feelings of sadness.

Art, music, and relaxation are gentle ways of going inside for healing but can also invite intrusive memories and feelings. It is very important that an adult trained to work with abused children guide the child through this book.

Encourage sports and other physical activities to help children release energy and stress. Children often have nightmares, sleep problems, and eating issues. Provide music and relaxation tapes to help them unwind before bedtime.

It is often difficult for children to trust adults after adults have abused them or failed to protect them. They may need their own space—but they will also need closeness.

As a means of surviving, children who have been abused often "side with" the abuser because that is the person with power. Children from violent homes have had poor models for anger management and self-control. They need education, support, and better adult models to avoid becoming the next generation of abusers.

Children who have been abused often feel hopeless, worthless, and powerless, and are unable to act in their own best interest. They need to be referred for specialized medical and psychological care. But children are very resilient, and many are able to thrive after traumatic experiences.

Many excellent books are available in bookstores and libraries with the age-appropriate education for anger management, self-control, and character development that these children need.

With help and support, victims can become survivors.

This book is intended to help children cope with the emotional aftermath of abuse by teaching them that

To children

This is your book. You will make it different from all other books by drawing your own thoughts and feelings. You do not need any special skills to illustrate the pages. Just use lines, shapes, and colors to draw the pictures that come into your head as you read the words on each page.

Begin with the first page and do the pages in order. An adult will help you with any words or pages you do not understand. You may share any thoughts and feelings you have with this adult as you work.

There may be pages in the book where you want to draw a picture about something you do not feel ready to talk about. That is okay. You can wait to talk about these pictures until you feel ready. Most children find that it is very helpful to share their work with a caring adult.

I hope you will have fun with this book. Sharing your problems and thoughts with others can help you feel better about yourself and the world.

Drawing can be fun. Draw some lines and shapes or just some silly colorful scribbles.

Children sometimes think scribbles are ugly, but scribbles can make pretty pictures, too.

Draw some scribbles inside and around each circle using bright colors. Add a green stem and leaves to make flowers. Draw a scribble line for grass.

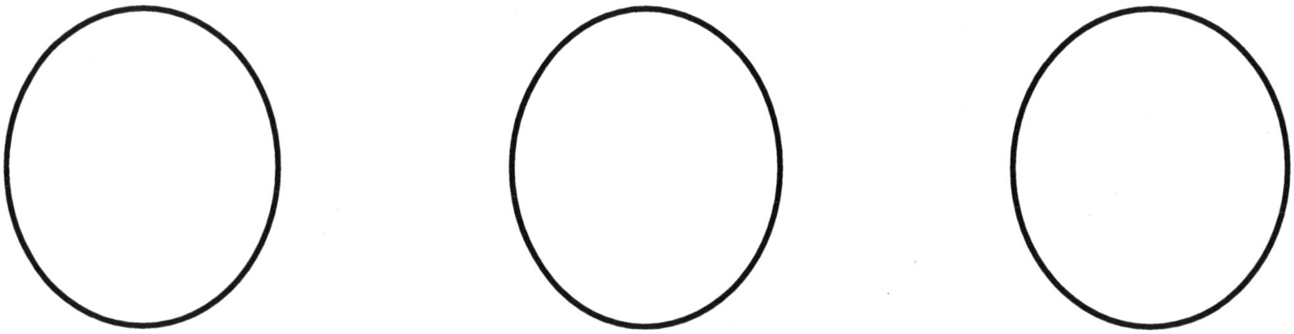

Add some sunshine and rain to help the flowers grow.

Flowers need a safe place to grow, like a garden or park or flower pot.

(Draw a safe place for flowers to grow. Add someone to take care of the flowers.)

Flowers are fragile. To grow well, they need care, food, and safety.

Children are fragile, too. They need a safe place to live and someone to love and care for them. They need healthy food to eat and clean, warm clothes to wear.

(Draw some things that children need.)

Children cannot take care of themselves. They need help from adults.

Some homes are full of anger and violence. Some people don't respect other people, animals, or things.

(Draw an angry home.)

Angry, violent homes are not safe places for children. People need to express anger in ways that do not hurt others or themselves.

Children are afraid to talk about some things that happen in their home.

(Draw something they could be afraid to talk about.)

Hearing or seeing loved ones hurt each other hurts children. Words can hurt as much as hitting.

Some people take their anger out on children and hit, push, or shove them. This is called physical abuse. Shouting, name-calling, put-downs, or unkind words can hurt too. This is called emotional abuse. Others may not give their children the things they need to be safe and healthy, like food and clothing. This is called neglect. Children who see or hear others being abused are harmed as well.

There are laws to protect children from all kinds of abuse.

Most children like good hugs and "good touch," but some adults play secret "bad touch" games with children. This is called sexual abuse. It makes no difference if a child like or hates these games. It is never the child's fault.

(Draw a picture of the way a child might feel about keeping these secrets.)

Adults know this is wrong and against the law. They are responsible and need to be punished.

Some adults do things that hurt children and make them think they are not loveable . . . but all children are loveable.

(Draw a loveable child.)

We do not always know why some adults hurt children, but we do know that it is never the child's fault.

Many children have suffered physical abuse, emotional abuse, sexual abuse, or neglect.

(Draw a picture of how children might feel.)

It is important for children to tell someone if they are abused. They need to make a plan to feel safe.

Adults may have big problems or worries. They may feel angry or upset. But it is not okay for grown-ups to hurt children even if they are upset.

(Draw some things that cause problems for adults.)

There are places to help adults until they are able to help themselves.

When adults learn self-control, they can help their children learn how to manage anger in ways that do not hurt others.

(Draw a picture of yourself with self-control.)

It will be a better world when people learn to help instead of hurt each other.

It is not a child's job to protect someone being abused. If someone is being abused, children can call 911 for help.

(Draw a picture of a safe place to go.)

Ignoring problems will not make them go away. Many problems get worse. When someone is being abused, it is important to call for help.

Many people care about children. Children often need help from others.

(List the names of people who can help you.)

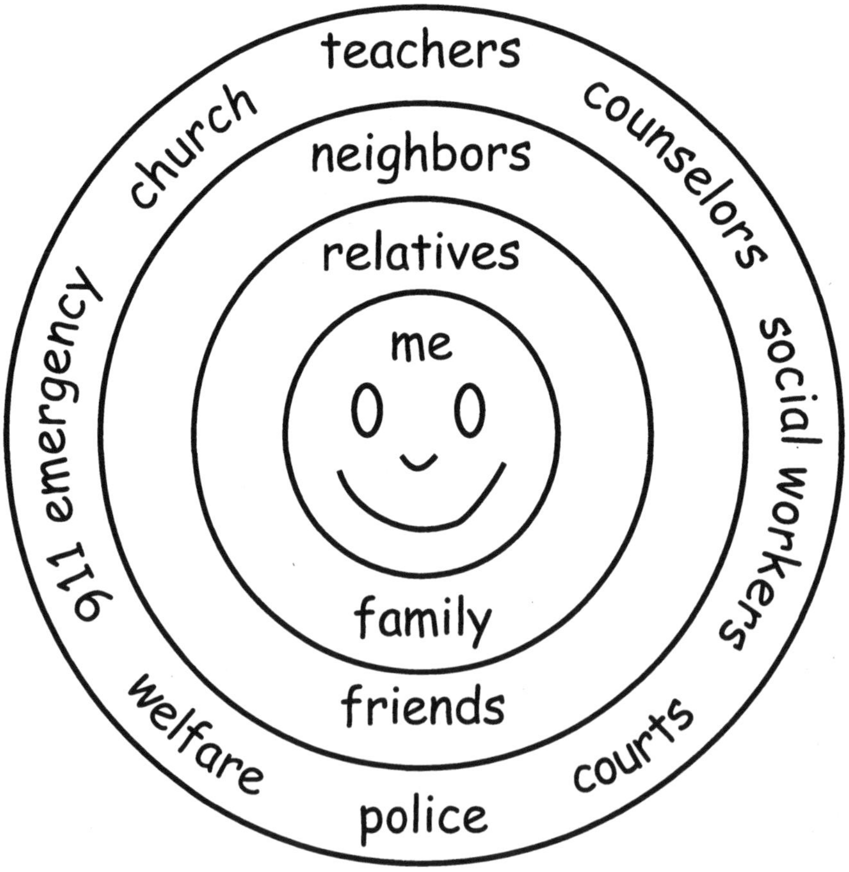

Children are important. They are the future of the world.

If children are abused in any way, laws are broken. Police or Child Welfare must be called to help children who are being abused.

(Draw a picture of someone who helps children.)

The police and Child Welfare will try to bring peace and keep children safe.

It may be necessary to have a judge in a court decide what is best for a child.

(Draw a picture of a courtroom.)

Going to court can be scary, but the adult is on trial, not the child.

Adults sometimes say a child is lying even though the child is telling the truth. Abuse is a difficult crime to work with.

(Draw a picture of how a child might feel.)

Children can be proud of doing something that is very hard to do.

When adults break the rules of the world, they may be sent to jail, even if the child does not want that to happen.

(Draw a picture you choose to draw.)

Children may feel safer if an adult goes to jail, but they may also feel sad. They may think it is their fault and feel guilty, but it is never the child's fault.

Children may need to be moved to a safer place to live until their parents are able to take better care of them.

(Draw a picture of a place that could take good care of children.)

This is very hard for children. They will have many feelings.

When children are abused, they may lose their trust in adults and their lives may change. When they lose things or when things change, they may have strong feelings. These feelings are called grief. Grief comes and goes like ocean waves.

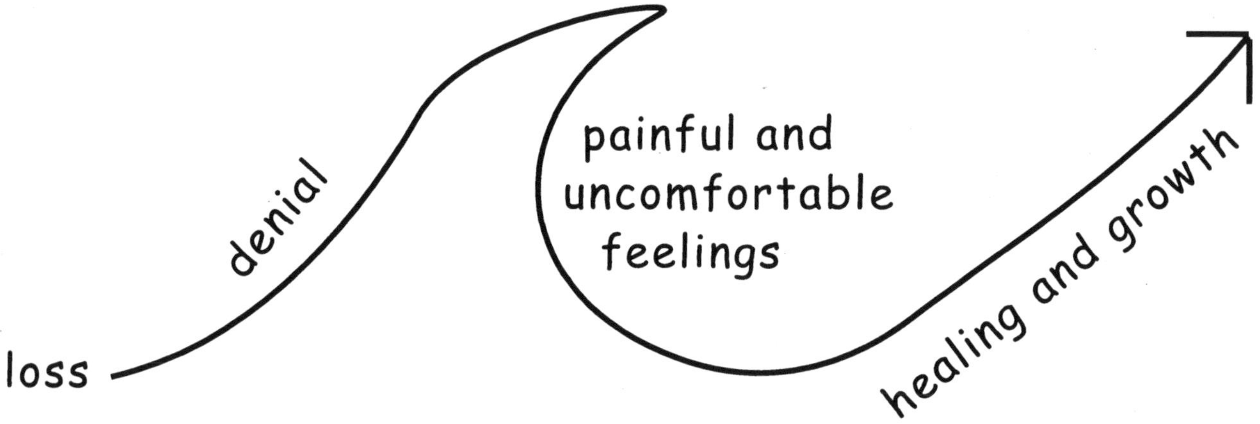

At first children may deny or try to hide their feelings of grief. With help they learn to understand and express their feelings so that they can heal their inner pain and grow stronger and wiser.

Children have many feelings. Sometimes they have so many feelings they feel overwhelmed.

(Use colors, lines, or shapes to show different feelings.)

anger	fear	happiness
shame	silliness	sadness

Everyone has all kinds of feelings. Feelings just happen.

Children may hide difficult feelings by pretending to feel something else. It is almost like wearing a mask.

(Draw and name some feelings and masks.)

a difficult feeling | a feeling mask to hide that feeling | how it feels under the mask

a difficult feeling | a feeling mask to hide that feeling | how it feels under the mask

Masks make it hard for others to get to know you and help you with your feelings.

Feelings are called feelings because you feel them someplace in your body.

(Close your eyes and think of a time when you had a strong feeling. Choose a color to show where you feel that feeling. Scribble that color next to the word below.)

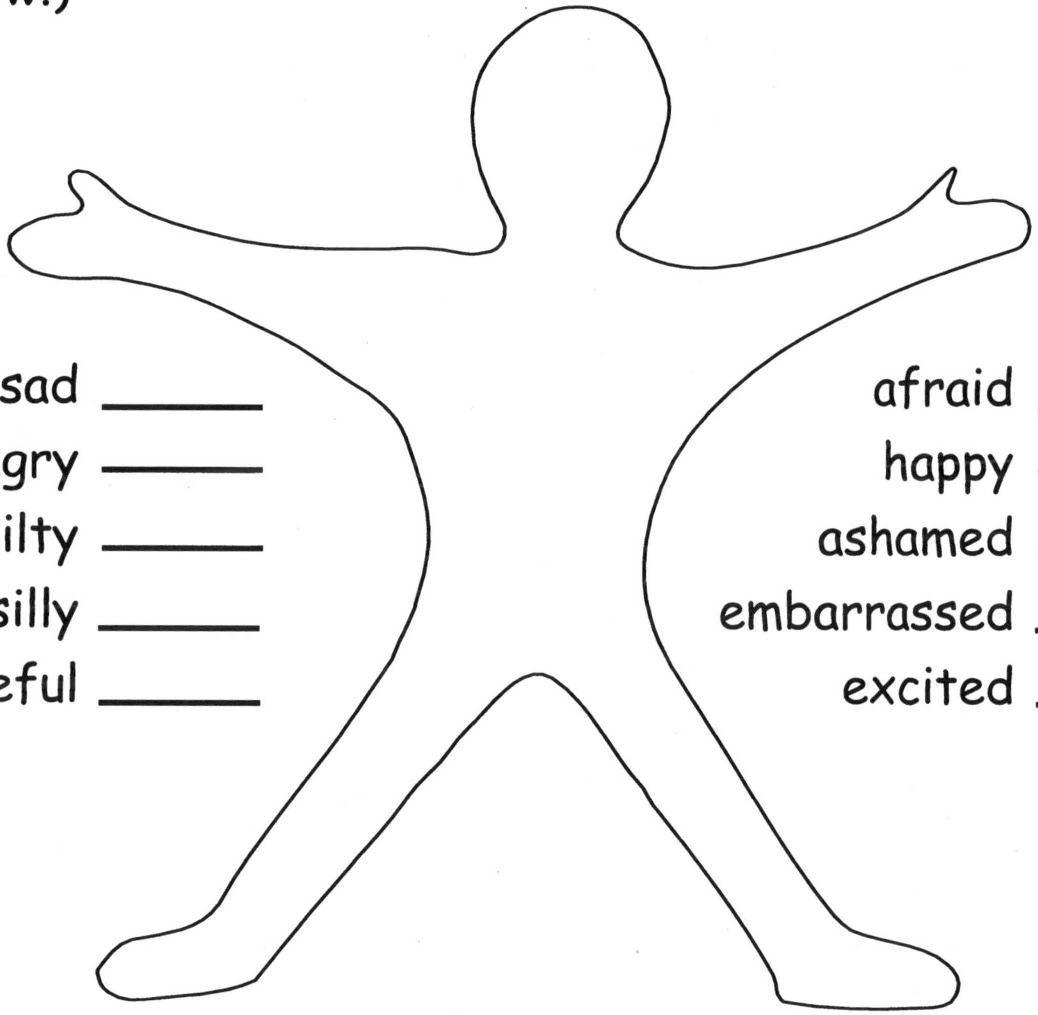

sad ______

angry ______

guilty ______

silly ______

hopeful ______

afraid ______

happy ______

ashamed ______

embarrassed ______

excited ______

All feelings are okay. Feelings change.

When feelings are kept stuffed inside, they can cause aches and pains.

(Use a crayon to color the places you get aches and pains.)

It is not healthy to deny feelings.

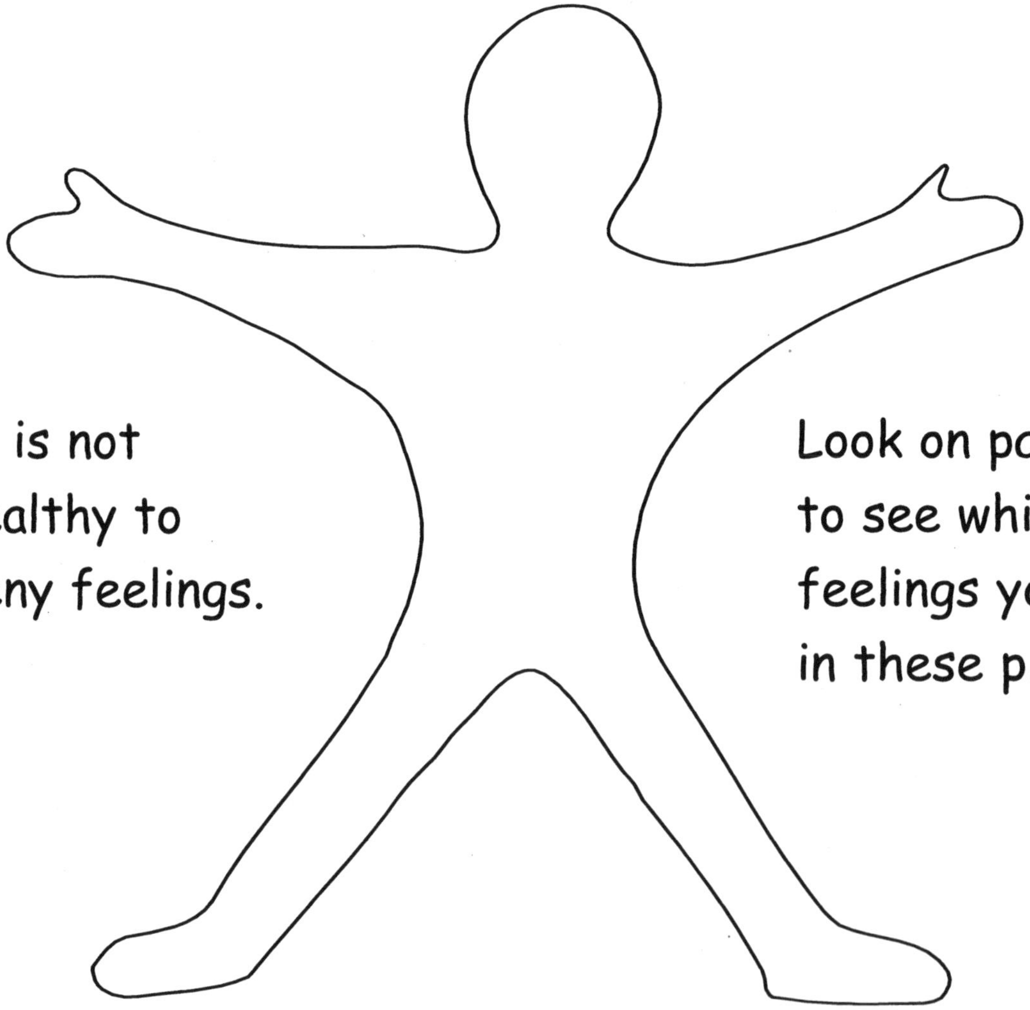

Look on page 23 to see which feelings you stuff in these places.

It is important to learn to let feelings out in okay ways.

Sometimes children feel guilty.

(Draw a picture of something children might feel guilty about.)

Children may think they caused the abuse, but they did not. They may think they can prevent abuse from happening, but they cannot. It helps to talk to someone when you feel guilty.

Unhappy children may break things or take things that do not belong to them.

(Draw a picture of something a child might do.)

Children need to learn to respect things they own and the things that belong to others.

Children may feel powerless and try to act tough or be mean just to feel stronger. They could hurt someone.

(Draw a picture of a bully.)

Thinking and brain power can be more powerful than muscle power.

Children can learn to relax when they feel themselves getting angry. Relaxing gives them time to cool down. Children can:

1. Count to ten.
2. Repeat to themselves: "I am upset, but I can handle this."
3. Relax their body like a rag doll, breathe out slowly, and let go of their anger.
4. Leave an angry situation and go listen to calm music while they draw or paint.
5. Bring a picture of a happier time to their mind.

6.

7.

8.

Calming thoughts and deep breathing can help children relax and make better choices.

Children who have been abused will have many feelings of anger. They can learn to let anger out in ways that will not hurt people or things. It is okay for children to:

1. Say "I'm angry because . . . ."
2. Stomp their feet.
3. Yell into a pillow or the shower.
4. Talk with someone about their problem.
5. Write an angry letter and tear it up.
6. Write angry thoughts in a journal.
7. Scribble on an old newspaper using many colors and feelings, scrunch the paper into a ball, and throw the ball at a blank wall.
8. Walk or run fast.

9.

10.

Children can choose what to do with their anger, but they are responsible for their behavior.

Sometimes children act silly and have trouble controlling their behavior because . . .

(Write or draw a picture to finish this sentence.)

Children may see hurtful behavior in their home, but they can learn to develop self-control, manage anger, and grow up to live a better life.

Draw a peaceful place where a family lives happily together.

Not all homes are violent places. Most homes are not violent.

Children have rights.

Children everywhere have the right to:

1. Be loved.
2. Have good food.
3. Have warm and clean clothing to wear.
4. Be treated with respect.
5. Live in a safe place.
6. Be safe from harm.
7. Live in a caring family and community.
8. Survive and thrive.

Children can learn to be strong and stand up for their rights.

This is my favorite kind of day.

(Draw a picture of the kind of day you enjoy.)

Weather changes all the time. Life often changes too.

There will be times for children who have been abused when they feel sad or bad inside. But there will also be many happy times ahead.

(Draw a picture of a happy time.)

Each day is a new beginning. Enjoy life!